# *Change Your Perce*

# *Change Your Perception*

© Mikel N Muse Creations
All Rights Reserved

ISBN 9798821169662

Published 2022

Find me on Instagram and Facebook

Mikelnmusewriting
@mikelnmusewriting

*Change Your Perception*

# The Motivational Guide to Hmmmmmmmm......... Change Your Perception

# Change Your Perception

*We are not trying to reinvent the wheel with this book. Instead, the intention is to take what you already know to be true and change how you see it. Everything in life is about how you choose to see it. There are so many things that are beyond the normal range of sight. As you look out of your window and gaze into the void of space. You see the trees in the distance, but do you see the way the sky wraps around them? The shades and hues of blue, white, and purple that make the skyline. Do you see the clouds as they form funny shapes or the way the birds fly in formation? There is always something you miss. Yet as you ponder how often did you miss these things you are already changing your perception. So, dig in and buckle up for this motivational guide in seeing things just a tad bit differently then what you are used to.*

## *Change Your Perception*

*The world is full of magic things, patiently waiting for our senses to grow sharper.*

*W.B. Yeats*

*Change the way you look at things and the things you look at change.*

*Wayne W Dyer*

## *Change Your Perception*

*Life is 10 percent what you make it,
and 90 percent how you take it.*


*Irving Berlin*


*All our knowledge has its origins in
our perception.*


*Leonardo da Vinci*

*Change Your Perception*

# The Motivational Guide to Hmmmmmmm........

# Change Your Perception

## *Change Your Perception*

*To every person, place, and thing that fueled the inspiration behind the words.*

*Happy Reading..............*

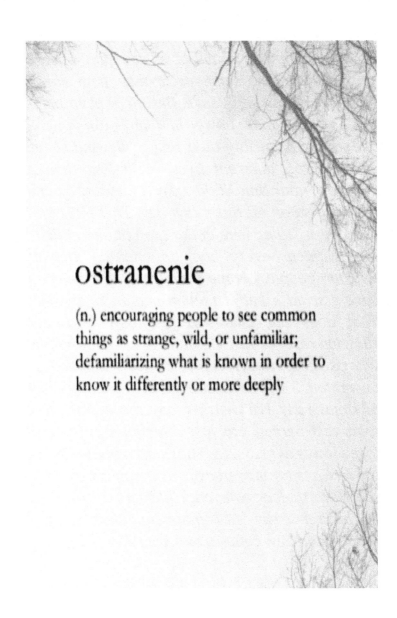

ostranenie

(n.) encouraging people to see common things as strange, wild, or unfamiliar; defamiliarizing what is known in order to know it differently or more deeply

# *Change Your Perception*

*As we face the destruction of society through the methodologies of war, poverty, hate, and violence. Let me just remind you. It takes you more energy and effort to hate someone or tear them down, then it does to simply love. But there is no man-made weapon more powerful than love. If you tell one stranger, you love them daily. You would have affected 365 different lives. With less than a minute of your time. If they pay it forward by one now and so on 60 times in a day. That is 21,900 people spreading love in the span of one hour. If that happens every hour in one day that is 525,006 people. Let me simplify. In one day you have started a half a million-person revolution. That does not factor in just how impactful showing care for just a minute is to an individual who is ready to give up. Who feels unloved or unwanted. 3 words most of us say meaninglessly 50 times a day. We love this song, those shoes, this food, that person, etc. Just remember in the end love always wins. So, why not start a revolution in the face of a tyranny none of us thought we'd ever see. Nevertheless, want our children to grow up in. As the French say " Et l'amour conquiert tout, pas vrai?" ( and love conquers all, right?)*

## Change Your Perception

Perfection is self-inflicted mental suicide. Perfection doesn't exist because it is perceived not obtainable. We reach so often for perceived things then wonder why we fall face first. Really in all honesty most of our lives are just our perception of one movie playing on a loop. Everyone has the same movie. It is why we cross the same people over and over. Lifetime after lifetime. The movie never changes. How we perceive it does. Look at your favorite book. If you read it happy, you perceive its words to feel you likewise. Yet if you are sad, those words resonate with you differently. The book is the same. Same pages and same words. That is how life is. One big movie, where we all have the same backdrop. We just all choose different ways to interact with it. Which then causes others to react as they perceive it. Leading to billions of different short films, that make up an anthology of our lives.

## Change Your Perception

*You are too good for everyone present. Only good enough for one's future and can't be forgotten in people's past. Universal paradox. We think we are nothing, yet we are all three at once every second of the day*

## Change Your Perception

*The center of a circle is empty. A circle with a twist is infinity. You only control what is in the boundaries of your circle. Everything outside of it is in the hands of the universe. The infinite universe that twists your circle to show you that you are infinite as well. Your soul, your spirit, and your energy all infinite. So why do you worry or stress? If you get it all wrong, there is always next time. Cut your losses and let the negative baggage go. Live, love, and enjoy the time you have left. Make the memories worth remembering and carrying into your next journey.*

## Change Your Perception

*Nothing to fear in life, because we all end up at the same place. No matter how careful you are. No matter how fast or slow you move. The race and the finish line are always the same. It is all about how you run the race. It is about the experiences you have throughout the journey. Remember it is never the start or the finish. It is always the journey. So, take in the scenery and smell the roses. Make the most out of every breath you have.*

## *Change Your Perception*

*Stop mistaking loneliness for love.
If you have to question it, then most
likely it is not love. Stop trying to
find yourself in others. Instead
learn to love yourself. Find peace in
your head and comfort in your soul.
No one will ever understand you
better then you. You cannot
properly love others until you
properly love yourself. Fact is you
spend the most time with yourself.
People come and go and, in the end,
you always have you. So, always be
the kindest to yourself.*

## Change Your Perception

*You there, yes you! You children of the moon. You gypsy spirits and druidic souls. The angel haired hipsters and purveyors of love. You amazing, beautiful, and enigmatic creatures. Created from energy, love, magic, and cosmic star dust. Stop dulling your finish to fit into a society driven by hate, greed, and destruction. Let your beautiful colors and light shine bright like a lighthouse in the fog. This world needs you to teach it how to love. To instruct them how to dig out that inner child buried in the rubble of normality. Remind them how to jump in puddles, dance in the rain, and count stars. You are never alone, as we are the majority. Everyone you come across is just like you in some way. They have just lost their ways. They need you to show them this amazingly beautiful universe again. You are a vital and integral part of the ultimate mission. That being the mission of love. A revolution needed to save us from our self-destructive ways.*

## *Change Your Perception*

*Change your habits:*

*Every day when you wake up say out loud one thing you are thankful for. Something different every day never the same thing. Do this for thirty days and then repeat.*

# Change Your Perception

*Your shadow is your darkness being seen. It is always with you. Always a part of you. You cannot have light without the dark. You cannot have happy without sad. Embrace all of who you are.*

# *Change Your Perception*

*If you come looking for me yesterday, you will not find me. For I no longer live there. If you come looking for me tomorrow, I will not be there. For tomorrow is too far away. Today is where I dwell. Learning from yesterday and preparing for tomorrow. Basking in the sun of now and singing the praises of in the moment.*

# Change Your Perception

*For so many great love stories are doomed to their surroundings. Drenched in the vernacular of the ignorance of their times. Covered in secrecy due to their nature. So shall there always be the need of societies example of pure true love. One with no need to hide or fall victim to the past's tragic short comings. A love to be shouted from a megaphone through the loudspeakers of the war-torn horizons. So that all may know its existence. Hear its passion and seek its place in each individual heart. That as the battle rages for meaningless treasures. The example alone will show the ultimate reward. Drop their misguided weapons and seek to love not to hate. Search not to conquer. Build up instead of tearing down. A love bread of the soul's desire to radiate its glow in an effort to change the future. Though it is romantic in nature it can be translated to all who pay attention and paid forward from every creed and nationality. For in a moment the world can change. It does so every day. Often times reporting only the negative to instill fear for controls purpose. What if that love was so powerful the only news to report is that one day the world stood still, and we all chose love?*

## *Change Your Perception*

*As day breaks in the distance. I watch the fog hover and dance on the water. The trees still desolate from winter showing signs of regrowth. The water ripples from the wind still winding from the passing storm. The slate gray sky gives way the power of the rising sun. Suddenly I realize that the storms will rage, but soon will pass. Everything must die in order to be reborn. That everything beautiful in the dark is more so in the light. I breathe in the crisp air letting it all go. Knowing today is a new day. I can make it anything I want, so I smile.*

## Change Your Perception

*Orphans in dystopia. Left to fend for themselves. Scared and alone clinging to a dirty bear. Food and love avoid them. They form a society in an effort to find some sort of support. Living off scraps left in a war-torn world. Did their parents die or just leave them? Will they see tomorrow? Will they ever be loved? Questions mount more than the security they need. Though easy to ignore sitting comfortably in your home. Surrounded in love and provisions. Throwing things away as if it were just a few bucks. Easier to ignore the facts of children left or adults who lost everything. Homelessness and abandonment are dystopia without it being in the future. While you struggle to understand someone's love be mindful. There are people wishing anyone would show them love over neglect. There are people who would wear those clothes you needlessly bought then discarded. Life isn't easy even more so to those who have nothing. Love is love and everyone needs it.*

# Change Your Perception

*What you see and judge me by is nothing but a woven tapestry. Made up of skin, hair, and cells. Attached to a fragile shell made of bone, muscles, and ligaments. It is merely just the casing to protect who I truly am. You judge me by my habits, traits, actions, and reactions. All stemming from a brain and a heart. Two muscles that operate the shell. Both replaceable and transplantable. Serving only the purpose to guide me around this big blue ball. It is not me. I am stardust and light. Magic and energy balled up into an irreplaceable sphere. I was created from shooting stars and fire. Wind, rain, rock, and ore. I am every chemical and that's why I react. I am every season and that is why I change. I am every wish and dream rolled up into an imperfect incantation. I am every one of you that judge me, and everyone that doesn't. For we all derive from the same exact starting point. From the same exact ingredients. Headed to same exact finish line. I may look different and act differently, but I am you and you are me. We are all made of love to be loved and to love each other. For just like time and space is infinite, so is love.*

## Change Your Perception

*Failure is not fully the opposite of success. In failure we grow and learn. It is a stepping stone on the road to success. The only true failure is never attempting anything at all. You miss one hundred percent of the shots you never take. For a bird has no idea what it is meant to be. Until forced from the nest to use its talents and gift to fly. Today is the day. Now is the time. This is the place. Stop putting off your success in fear of your failure. Just remember that danger is real, but fear is chosen reaction.*

## *Change Your Perception*

*Life is about learning to ride the wave. Sometimes you are scared and other times brave. There is an array of colors from red to white. Even the shades of black that make up the night. Life is not always about having fun. Some days are grey with no signs of the sun. The darkness helps us to appreciate. That happiness can always be found in any state. Once we learn the ways to survive the storm. From every shooting star another star is born. What is meant to be will always find a way. What is destined to leave will never stay. The key is embracing the highs and lows of life. Remembering that overthinking only brings forth strife. Do not let the negative dictate the way you perceive. Be positive and know success is coming if you will only just believe.*

*PA*

## Change Your Perception

*Time is infinite. So why would life end with death? Does the moon and sun not set then rise again? Do the trees and bushes not shed their liveliness to become barren and bloom again? Will not a star shoot across the sky leaving trails of dust that still illuminate? Death is merely the ability to be reborn and start anew. We all die hundreds of times in life. Each time feeling as if we will never recover. Yet we all emerge like the phoenix from the ashes. Newly reborn to start a fresh. To soar in the wind and become everything we were not before.*

# Change Your Perception

*Love. The most chaotic of emotions. Whether we speak of superficial love such as the feelings towards food, hobbies, or music. To the unconditional form between a parent and their child or even their pet. Oh, but romantic love, is the most chaotic of all. It will drive your brain insane, as you in mere minutes feel every overwhelming emotion and feeling at once. Like being bound to the knife throwers pinwheel spinning uncontrollably at 20 mph. Daggers flying from every direction as the sound of broken boards drive the brain to snap. As the wheel stops you hope the wounds are minimal and the bleeding ceases. Regardless of what range of love we speak of the extremities of it are very real. A parent when facing the option would storm the gates of the realm of hell. No weapons just a soul filled with love and a brain full of rage to protect their child. A pet owner would sacrifice their health in times of poverty to assure their fur baby ate. Even if they didn't get to. Wars are fought and lives lost over the love of an idea or country. A soul connected to another bound with the threads of love would drive hours to have just half a day with their soul's counterbalance. Even those destroyed and hardened hearts need love.*

## Change Your Perception

*They may say they are better off alone then be hurt again, but that's not true. To spend a life without love is like walking death row only at the time to be strapped to the table. Were thrown into solitary confinement. To waste and rot away longing for the lethal injection. It is in our celestial and chemical make up to need love. It is a basic love. A soul with no love will perish way before a body with little nourishment. The mental break would send vibrations to end it all. When all you hear is the disturbing sound of silence and you can hear the shadows move. We are predisposed to need each other. To need companionship. To need love. The energy you harness can save a life and just a symbol of love. Even to a stranger can move the world. Sending it spinning in a completely different direction. What if we all loved more then we complained or hated? In the immortal words of Sam Cooke "But I do know that I love you, and I know that if you love me too. What a wonderful world this would be."*

# *Change Your Perception*

*Constant knowledge and growth are essential. Only when you stop learning do you stop living. You can exist but not live. You can love but never be in it. It's the universes ultimate paradox. You can be while never fully being, a rather scary thought.*

## Change Your Perception

*Change your habits:*

*Go outside and look at one thing of nature. Now close your eyes and take a few deep breaths. When you open your eyes see how many things around that object you now see. Changing your perception will train your eyes and brain to see beyond just the norm.*

## *Change Your Perception*

*A tree doesn't cower in fear of the changing of the seasons. Knowing as winter draws nigh what makes them aesthetic and beautiful must die. In order to welcome new life and rebirth in the spring. So why should you fear the death of those things in your life that have become stale or unhealthy? If it no longer adds to your happiness or progress shed, it like the leaves in the fall winds. Allow yourself to be ready for the beauty of blossoming and necessary growth in your life. Don't fear change. Fear staying the same as everything else changes around you.*

# *Change Your Perception*

*How can you leave, when you won't use the
door?*
*How can you dance, when you never get on
the floor?*
*How can you shine, when you're afraid of the
dark?*
*How do you start the fire, when you won't be
the spark?*
*How can you succeed, when you put the horse
before the cart?*
*How can you win the race, when you won't
even start?*
*Only thing standing in your way is you.*
*Keeping you from what you need to do.*
*Believe in yourself, that's the only way.*
*Pay no attention to what others say.*
*Walk to the ledge, jump... then exhale.*
*Prove them all wrong when you prevail.*

## *Change Your Perception*

*The enigmatic war of attrition between heart and soul. There will never be a winner. The heart it longs for what it feels. Yet the soul feels deeper than anything the heart can imagine. There you find the constant battle between love and true love. You see you begin the reckless journey to love with the brain. You stimulate every attribute about someone. How their laugh makes you smile. Ping. How their eyes melt your heart. Ping. How conversation stimulates both mind and heart. Ping. All of a sudden shock and awe. The battle has begun. The heart becomes attached and longing sets in. To hear their voice or to be near them. To constantly think about them. What is transposed as butterflies in your stomach? What feels like a violinist playing their symphony on the strings attached to your heart. You jump mindlessly. Your brain now detached from the battle watches as you jump. Falling, tumbling, soaring into love. Knowing not if there is a net to catch you. Thinking not at all about your reserves. Then crash....*

## Change Your Perception

*You are swimming in the pools of lust... desire... love... Floating as if nothing could ever go wrong. Blissfully coasting on the waves and crashing into the walls of the heart. Blinded by the beautiful hues of loves fog. Suddenly you feel it tugging on you from below. The pull like a magnetic field. Drawing you under. You plunge deeper into loves pools. Diving to find that pull. What was it? Where is it now? The soul it beckons like a sonar wave reverberating against the rocks. The vibrant ping leading you to its location. Frantically you swim deeper and deeper. Then as you hit the dark yet cool floor of loves ocean. You see the light refracting through blackened waters. A signal leading beyond the flooring. You feel you can get no closer, yet you find yourself digging anyway. Feverishly tunneling, the light gets brighter. Unsure you take leave into the hole you've created until you are standing. Flat footed on solid ground staring mindlessly at a ball. A ball of energy and light spinning both clockwise and counterclockwise in unison.*

## Change Your Perception

*You reach slowly towards it, and you are instantly sucked in. Into a space free of gravity. Glimmering like stars in the sky. Floating weightless and feeling every single emotion at once. Waves of emotions crashing over you. Unexplained feelings of doubt, worry, and fear mingle with euphoric retorts. Suddenly when you think it cannot get more intense the dance begins. A tango between two partners similar in nature, yet oh so very different. Love spinning you around on a glass surfaced floor. Twisting and turning into true loves grasp. Firmly on your waist as to guide your every step. The heart pulling you away as the soul entrances you with its seductive pull. Back and forth attacks are taken as you play both pawn and rook. The beauty of love crashes against the realness of the soul's home like feel. Like fighting a current you frantically try to swim away, but to no avail. The rising of loves tide simultaneously beats against the souls downward pull. Then suddenly silence... You float towards the surface lifeless and weightless.*

# *Change Your Perception*

As you reach the crest where light crashes against the water you can finally breathe. You swim to the shore of the brains beach. Suddenly the war that rages inside of you reaches the reasoning of the brain. Questions fly like birds migrating for the winter. Trying to rationalize everything you've experienced and what it all means. Where do you go from here, and what is real? Like a tornado you are swept up and entangled in every emotion. Winds ripping at the very core. Violently crashing you against reason and understanding. Confusion becomes your sanctity, and you stare mind numbingly into space. Oh, to be in love, and you wonder why people in love look so exhausted...

# *Change Your Perception*

*You can fall apart and still help others. It's often easier to help others then to deal with your own issues. You get wrapped up in others, and by the time your situations catch up. They are far too much to handle. Every coin has a flip side. All good comes with bad, and vice versa. When you focus too much on one or the other. You are blindsided by what you ignore. Be kind to others but remember to be kind to yourself as well. We are all connected, and while you may be having a string of bad luck. Someone you are connected to is having good. So celebrate with them, because when they are dealing with the bad you will have the good. If you are awake on average 16 hours a day you are also awake 3,600 minutes which equates to 57,600 seconds. Every decision you make takes 1 second. It will affect at least 10 people at a time. Therefore your 57,600 decisions will also be 576,000 reactions. Don't be so hard on yourself for making mistakes. Don't be so harsh on those making mistakes. Remember a circle is empty until you twist it. We all live the circle of life and when twisted it makes infinity. We are infinitely connected and there are infinite possibilities.*

*Breathe and love one another. The only thing as infinite as time is love.*

## Change Your Perception

*Acceptance is the hardest part. For these two facts always remain. People come and they will go.*

*Time does not stop, and life does go on. No matter what these things do not change. How long will you lose refusing to let go?*

# *Change Your Perception*

*What's wrong with these people you ask?*
*Why is there so much anger and hate?*
*Why are kids so detached and desensitized?*
*Our society has become the failed experiment of the*
*machine. We the cogs. Numbered and easily replaced.*
*Social anxiety has become the new hyperactivity. Big*
*pharm allows for solutions to the blanket diagnosis of*
*ADD/ADHD. Trained well educated professionals*
*selling their souls for the all mighty dollar. Can't or*
*don't want to figure out what's really going on?*
*Throw these pills and those diagnoses at them. Smile*
*and cash the check. Our world controlled,*
*manipulated, and fully functional with applications*
*on a cell phone. Why do kids struggle? Why do people*
*not get along? Simple. You can live your life from the*
*safety and sanctuary of your own home. Online jobs*
*remove adult interaction. Music, videos, and games*
*replace outdoor activities. You can buy your food and*
*have it delivered, cooked or uncooked to your door.*
*Social media allows you to interact with millions of*
*people every day. You can be whomever you choose.*
*Look any way a filter allows. Many have more friends*
*online then in person. Meeting new people relegated*
*to dating sites. Ones that for the most part start off as*
*harmless. Then slowly become hook up sites in the*
*blink of an eye. You can get ordained, married, and*
*divorced in your living room. Welcome to what was*
*called mind control in the 80's. Drug and alcohol*
*addiction pale in comparison to technology*
*addiction. People text each other from the other*
*room.*

# *Change Your Perception*

*No need to get up and walk the 15ft to the other room. You can get every bit of someone's information for the low cost of $9.99 a month or $115 a year. People walk into traffic never looking up. Drive down the street the same way. Our society has reverted to Neanderthal like interaction while progressing to cars that park and drive themselves. Some call it convenience, but I ask what convenience? So, you can spend more time never experiencing real life. The beauty of a sunset. The magic of counting stars and naming them. Get-togethers full of laughter. You can't experience life never looking up. Our children are not messed up just lost. We accept the job of molding them to be ready for real life. Yet so many enter adulthood not having a clue how to handle it. The what-ifs and possibilities overwhelm them to the point of panic attacks. We babysit them with television, games, and cell phones. Our leaders have failed us, but we are failing the next generation. Eventually the idea of intelligence will exist only in the computer brains of AI. Welcome to the thunder dome hope you are ready for what we all have created.*

## Change Your Perception

*Change your habits:*

*As you drive to work or have your morning cup of coffee. Simply say to yourself today is going to be a great day. Training your brain to think positively rather than being pessimistic will put positive energy into the universe.*

## Change Your Perception

*The key to happiness is to think and imagine in vivid color. Love in black and white, move so fast problems can never catch you.*

# *Change Your Perception*

*We are predisposed to think of life in the terms of years. We judge life based on how long someone lives. If someone under thirty dies everyone says "they died so young" or "they had their whole life ahead of them." Yet when someone over seventy dies it's " they have seen so much" or they've lived a good life." Life lived is not about years. I know kids at twelve that have been further and have seen more then I will by seventy. Life is a labyrinth. We all have purposes and lessons to learn in this lifetime. The end goal is to make it out and back home. Where you are one with everything and you are everything. Some figure it out faster and leave faster. Onto the next life. Others of us hit every dead end and wall along the way. There are others who know the way, yet they take their time. Age has no variance on completion. The issue is how our brains view mortality. It is common thought that someone late in life who has seen the world and accomplished so much has indeed lived a fuller life then a child. I disagree.*

## Change Your Perception

*Children live every day to the fullest with no fear of there even being a tomorrow. Did you worry about college when you were nine on a Friday night? All you thought about was the big bowl of cereal Saturday morning and watching cartoons. While watching cartoons did you think about your career and salary potential? Nope, you thought about playing outside with your friends. It's not until you hit junior high you are force fed the way life goes. You are taught college is next, then a career, marriage, family, home, vacation, 401k, retirement, etc. That's when you stop living every day to the fullest and begin the mind-numbing dance of what life is about. Change your perception. Find your inner child and live every day to its fullest. You may not travel the world or have the most luxurious lifestyle, but I promise you will enjoy living life again. You will stop counting years and start counting moments*

## *Change Your Perception*

*Goals are like dandelions.*
*You wish and think them to existence.*
*Your effort is the wind taking the seeds.*
*They float and plant into your pathway.*
*They grow into fruition then bloom. You*
*pick another and repeat...*

## Change Your Perception

*The hardest thing to learn in life is to be able to decipher between what you want and what you need. Learn to want what you need, and life becomes that much easier...*

## Change Your Perception

*Without chaos there is no peace, nor is there change. So, embrace the chaos. Don't run or hide from it. You see we learn from it. It teaches us when to fight and what to fight for. It teaches us to appreciate the calm. It makes us stronger as we come out the other side. Just remember everything has a counterbalance. When it is all going well for you it is chaotic and falling apart for someone else. Your time will come, so show patience and love. Do so for no gain of your own. It's the universe's way of teaching us to watch out for in each other. A smile or a joke in a time of inner turmoil can change the course way more than pity.*

## Change Your Perception

*Run, run little rabbit.*
*In and out of your bunny holes.*
*Running, hopping, bouncing*
*uncertain.*
*Anxiously looking side to side.*
*What is life? Where do I go?*
*Stop.... breathe.... focus....*
*Check the clock. Time flows the*
*same...*
*Answers come as they should.*
*Just remember in the end.*
*We are all a little mad here....*

# *Change Your Perception*

*I am a time bomb. Tick.*
*Self-doubt and self-destructive. Tick. Tick.*
*Over thinking and over analyzing. Tick. Tick.*
*Tick.*
*Tearing myself apart. Tick. Tick. Tick. Tick....*

*BOOOOM!*


*I crawl into my self-isolating shell.*
*The universe whispers... let go....*
*Nervously, anxiously, uncertain I rock.*
*Space is close I can't breathe. Help...*

*BOOOOM!!*


*I am a butterfly floating on the breeze.*
*Not a worry. Not a care. Not a trouble*
*Beautifully me. Perfectly imperfect.*
*Free to be whatever. Surrounded by light.*

## Change Your Perception

*We are all stardust, magic, and energy. Tucked safely into a flesh covered body. We return to the universe as shooting stars and rainbows. We are all the beauty of the universe wrapped in unique packages.*

## *Change Your Perception*

*Change your habits:*

*Look in the mirror and say something nice to yourself. You are both your biggest fan and worst enemy at the same time. So, why not focus more on being your biggest fan?*

# *Change Your Perception*

*Change your perception and your approach*

*Instead of seeing her looks see her soul.*

*Instead of craving her kiss crave her essence.*

*Instead of admiring her figure admire her spirit.*

*Instead of worshiping her body worship her mind.*

*Instead of asking for sex listen to her passion.*

*She is not a trophy to be owned. She is not an object to be claimed. She is a celestial being made of energy and light way beyond anything you can imagine. She will change your life. Know her worth and celebrate the beauty that never fades...*

# Change Your Perception

*Space is infinite. It surrounds everything. Billions of stars twinkle like perfect night lights in it. The sky hangs and cries from it. The sun shines in the day and the moon at night illuminating it. It is in the break of a song. Writers have penned scripts and books about it. Countries and nations have sent beings into it in the name of discovery. It exists between lives, hearts, souls, and beings. Still no matter what encompasses it space still exists. It still fills the holes between everything. A perfect infinite existence much like time. Time exists and continues infinitely. We claim to use it, waste it, chase it, and long for it. Still, it is always there. Our minds struggle to perceive infinite things. Objects, beings, and anything we can not physically see. If we cannot touch it or hold it, how can we agree it exists? The universe, time, and space will forever be here no matter what form or body your soul inhabits. You can call it magic, illusion, or madness. How else do you explain connections to people? You come across someone you've as far as you know never met. Yet one word in it feels as you've always known them. Those people who see through all the masks you wear to appease society. Hiding your true form for fear of being an outcast.*

# Change Your Perception

*You are too short, too fat, too ugly, too crazy, so on and so forth. So, we mask up to hide what isn't appealing to others and act as if we are someone else to fit in. A world full of actors and actresses aiming to win an award once they get, they realize they never wanted. To what sacrifice other than your mental stability? I look up at the moon and I see its phases. We are much like the moon. Very little exposed just a fragment of light when we first meet people. As our lives rotate, we slowly show more fragments and light. Until we are fully exposed in all our majestic form hoping to be appreciated for more than one day. Much like the seasons our attitudes adapt to form weather patterns. Our souls give off warmth like the summer. Burning hot and on fire when in love. As it fades, we become fall. The leaves slowly fall as the beautiful colors fade to show the barren existence of the shell leaves once covered. Leading to the cold shivering winter. Ice cold hearts longing for our spring. When we will thaw and blossom to try and love again. Still don't believe in the infinity of time, space, or the universe?*

## Change Your Perception

*Don't fear the darkness. If not for it the moon and stars would not shine as they do. There is beauty in the darkness.*

## Change Your Perception

*Indulge your spirit and embrace your energy. Listen to your soul's cry to evolve and grow. Open your eyes and see everything around you. Value heartbreak so you can fully love again. Elevate your self-worth because you are truly amazing. Yearn for change as it's essential in life. Observe the signs, the universe is speaking. Utilize your time and make the best of every day. Remember a butterfly did not start out as beautiful. It had to crawl on its belly as a caterpillar first. Then wrap itself up in a chrysalis before emerging as a beautiful creature.*

JM

## Change Your Perception

*In a world of instant gratification be a rebel and choose patience. It may be a forgotten virtue, but it still pays dividends.*

*PA*

## Change Your Perception

*You do not have to find yourself. You have to accept yourself. Wipe the mirror clean and realize everything you have always wanted to be. It has been inside you all along. Love and believe in yourself. Only then will you finally be fully yourself.*

# *Change Your Perception*

*Don't let the pebbles of people's opinions trip you on the rocky road to self-discovery.*

## Change Your Perception

*No one is better at being you then you. If anyone could be you there would be no reason for you to be here. Fact is we are all created uniquely different for the sole purpose of effecting this world as ourselves. So, stop trying to be like everyone else. Stop comparing yourself to everyone else. Most importantly stop beating yourself up for being you. You are a flesh covered ball of light, energy, spirit, beauty, and most importantly love. Stop saying I don't deserve this or that. Stop saying I won't ever have this or that. Trade pessimism for positivity. Not one person can dance like you, write like you, sing like you, and so on. Shine your light and allow yourself to take all the things right in front of your face. Stop looking down because there is a whole lot going on that you are missing. Look beyond your blinders and see the magic, beauty, and amazing colors and sounds of this universe. Just remember if you don't get it right this time you will have a next time. The universe is infinite therefore so are our spirits. We cannot be less then what we derive from. That is impossible...*

# *Change Your Perception*

*When you bring negative energy from your past into your future it's self-sabotage. You can't grow in a bed of thorns and weeds. You have to continually replant yourself in fertile soil.*

# Change Your Perception

*Stop using the word never when it comes to self-love or healing. Saying things like I will never heal from this. I will never be as good looking as them. I will never have their body. I will never trust or love again. Just those few words are enough negativity to alter your course. Always be aware you are where you are supposed to be and learning what you need to learn. Though the lesson may be a tough one. All lessons are meant for self-growth. You are exactly who you are supposed to be. Unique and special. The universe has had a plan for you all along. Those intuitions you ignored caused detours on your path. That is not the universes fault it is yours. Practice accountability. Remind yourself daily all emotional responses are your choice.*

*No one can make you mad, happy, sad, or feel hurt. Those are your chosen reactions to someone's actions. Most of the time they could care less how it affects you, so why sacrifice your peace? Remember every word you speak even alone is heard.*

# Change Your Perception

So, while you beat yourself up in private the universe hears your negativity.

Therefore, it gives negativity in return.

If you tell yourself consistently you are alone in the dark.

 You will never realize you are standing in the light. You think you are stuck in the storm when in all actuality you've beaten the storm. You just refuse to see that positivity. Be kind to others, but way more kind to yourself. People come and they go. In the end you always have you. You are always with you. So, why treat everyone else as more important than the one entity that never leaves you no matter what?

## *Change Your Perception*

*A bird is dropped from the nest once the mother believes it is ready to fly. Knowing if the baby doesn't flap its wings and use what nature gave it. The baby would not survive the fall. Still the mother pushes the child knowing it will be okay. It is time to jump. The universe is the mother bird and we the babies. It prepares us for our moment to jump. When it knows we are ready it gives the slightest nudge and off the cliff we go. Knowing all along we were ready to spread our wings and fly. Believe in the jump. Have faith in your wings. Know if the universe says you are ready. Well, then surely you are.*

JM

## Change Your Perception

*Change your habits:*

*Choose something you really want within reason. Instead of just going out and buying it. Make a plan. Figure out how much it will cost and divide it by four or eight. Taking a little bit every week out and saving towards that item. Not only do you reward yourself for hard work well done, but you set a goal and reached it. Now go set another and do not stop.*

# Change Your Perception

*For selv i nederlag vant han fortsatt. Kampen hans inspirerte andre til å kjempe. Hans styrke ga de svake makt. Mest av alt inspirerte hans kjærlighet til ideene hans andre til å drømme.*

*Translation:*

*For even in defeat, he still won. His struggle inspired others to fight. His strength gave the weak power. Most of all, his love for his ideas inspired others to dream.*

## Change Your Perception

*It takes a lot of courage to piece yourself together and carry on once broken. When all you want to do is fall apart and hide. Be kind because you have no idea who's going through what.*

*Everyone has endured some sort of tragedy or situation that has left them shattered into a million pieces. They all walk amongst you wearing their masks and smiles to hide the hurt and pain.*

*Remember a few uplifting words can be enough for someone to find the strength to carry on.*

*PA*

# Change Your Perception

An artist's depiction is merely their perception of what they see. You see a sundae when they see a cupcake. Look at Van Gough's starry night. He simply saw the stars covering the blanketed sky. His perception and interpretation have become one of the most used pieces of artwork in history. Though he lived and died poor. He saw beyond the world's perception of what the night looked like. Many a rich man will look up and see white spots on a black sky. Many a dreamer will spend all night counting billions of specks of stardust. Perception is everything. It is not only what you see it is what you feel. Instead of accepting what you see look beyond it. See from another's point of view. Open your mind to the possibilities you have in the past ignored.

JM

## Change Your Perception

*Fall in love with the moments not the time. For in the moments, you find joy and life. Time flies and there is always wonder. Where did it all go and why did I waste it? Yet in the moments that is where you get lost. You remember the feelings and the reactions. You remember the people and the places. Time is most definitely eternal. Always looping over and over. Those moments make time relevant and worthwhile.*

## Change Your Perception

*When will you all see we are all fragments of a perfect love? When will you stop surrounding yourselves with people that aren't like minded? How much longer will you self-destruct and self-depreciate yourself. Thinking I wish I were as smart as this person. I wish I could sing like them or write like him/her. The universe put you here to do wonderful things. Better yet, the same things as those people you worship like false God's. We all have the capability to achieve the same things anyone else has or will. Be it past, present, or future. Do you know what made what we see as the greatest minds ever so great? Their drive to be surrounded with others that would help them see differently from what they already did. Think differently and to have a consistently different opinion in their ear. They craved knowledge and growth. If you can think and form an opinion, you are a philosopher. If you can write down words that have meaning you are a writer. If you can draw even stick figures you are an artist.*

# Change Your Perception

*Stop setting yourself up for failure. Stop surrounding yourself with people that think like you do. Stop seeing things as always, exactly the same. Find those energies and minds that see things differently than you do. Force yourself to see it their way then find another perception. Your energy and your spirit crave these challenges. Find those souls that dance in the fields. Those angel haired hipsters writing about the stars. Find those outcasts that refuse to color on the page given to them. Screw the lines they make the world their canvas. The reason these people are not like you is because they refuse to conform to the thought this is how you are supposed to act. We live the same life. Everyone deals with life and death. We all work and slave to the point of depression. We all fight the darkness and until we do, we never appreciate the light. We all fall, and we all fail. We all succeed, and we all overachieve. Their situations may be different and based on your choices their path may wind more. Still, we all come from nothing to return to nothing.*

## Change Your Perception

*We all are love, made from love, and return to love. Not one person you meet can give you a definitive answer on after life. We do not know everything, nor will we ever. Why would you want to? Why watch a movie if you know the ending? There is no anticipation. Stop waiting for life to show you the way and blaze your own trail. Scoop up some of those weirdos you pass, and I promise you when you return. You will not be the same person. Challenge yourself to see things differently every day.*

*Find energies above yours so you strive to plug in every day and refuse the energies that do not meet yours. You are uniquely and unequivocally beautiful spectral anomalies. No one is you and you can never be anyone else. Own that and refuse to let a world that refuses to plug into the infinite universe tell you any different.*

# *Change Your Perception*

*What if everything is love? Meaning what if at the beginning of time we originated from one all-encompassing love. On our first lifetime we broke off as a piece of that love with a mission. That mission being to live a lifetime growing that love here on this earth. So, when you returned spectrally to the all-encompassing love you brought back more than you left with. Continuing to grow it lifetime after lifetime. That would mean we are all created from love. Made to love. Driven to find and share love. Then to return to love until you start the cycle again. A never-ending cycle for a never-ending universe. That would also mean every decision and mistake you have made makes absolutely no difference. So, you can stop beating yourself up. Every unhealthy or toxic relationship is unimportant. The only thing that matters in the end is the main mission of love. Imagine if you got yourself completely out of the way, and just did the one thing you were created to do. Just love. Love yourself, love other people, love life. Just love.*

# Change Your Perception

*How is it that one of the most beautiful times of the year is when everything is dying? In fall we watch the foliage of trees go from green to vibrant colors of orange, yellow, and red. Essentially going from thriving and alive to the rapid aging until they fall on the ground. Leaving the trees bare and barren. We celebrate the change of weather as it goes from hot and humid to chilly and breezy. We trade pools and beaches for weekend drives through the mountains and bonfires. We exchange beach balls for pumpkins and bathing suits for costumes. We welcome the fall like an old friend knowing it is just the rotation of the year. Every year has its seasons and this one tends to be a favorite. It is a perfect transition as many anticipate the holidays where we celebrate with family and friends. Funny how we welcome this in the all-encompassing knowledge of what it means, yet in life it is completely different. In life we do not celebrate death we mourn it.*

## Change Your Perception

*Instead of celebrating the life of someone we fixate on the sadness of them no longer being here. Yet all that is gone is their earthly body. The form you can see, touch, kiss, and hold. The essence of that individual is still very much alive. The spirit still lives and breathes in everything they did and taught us. Maybe it is in art form such as writing or painting. Could be in the lessons they taught us about life and love. Still, it can be as simple as the joys they found in animals or just life in general. We get so wrapped up in the word death. That it means gone forever. The word eternity means infinite or unending time. Never has it been said the human body is infinite. No one ever says my body will live for an eternity. We have all heard though that their spirit lives on for eternity. The soul is an infinite manifestation that cannot be destroyed. Therefore, meaning that a person's body will perish yet the soul will live on forever. That is hard to accept for most. It has been hard for me to swallow for sure.*

## *Change Your Perception*

*All though difficult as it may be to set aside the longing to see or talk to someone that has passed on. To celebrate their soul and the contributions it had and still has in life seems so much better. It not only keep their memory alive, but it also pays homage to the spirit they breathed into life. Death is hard to deal with on one end yet easy to celebrate when not talking about people. When in all honesty what we struggle to accept and come to grips with is reality. The reality that you cannot just call that person up or go to see them. What became normality and what we took for granted, because as humans we all do it. The person we thought would always be there is not there anymore. The reality it is impossible to knock on the door and give them a kiss or a hug. You cannot just dance to your favorite song or eat your favorite meal anymore. As sad as that thought is even sadder is the thought their spirit is still here, and we still take it for granted. We can still dance and sing.*

# Change Your Perception

*We can still enjoy that meal or talk all we want. Their spirit can still hear, and you know that because you feel it. You know when that song plays, and you get goose bumps it is them saying I hear it too. When you talk into space and feel comfort it is them saying I'm listening. When you close your eyes and feel warm when you see them. They are saying I am here. The first step is always the hardest on any journey. Especially when you were sure that person would be walking with you. Yet it is the most important. Not to move on as if they never existed, but to start the new journey. A voyage that they will still take with you every step of the way. Open your minds to more than reality. Allow yourself to see past the blinders. The universe is an amazing thing. It gives us everything we need and everyone. It is infinite and never-ending. As are we the spectral beings that inhabit flesh for only short periods of time. Then onto the next timeline to do it again. Always learning and growing. Best of all always existing.*

## *Change Your Perception*

*Change your habits:*

*Take time for just you. Do something you love to do. Read a book or take a walk. Go to your favorite store and just roam. Whatever brings you peace. Just do it alone. Take the time you block off to collect your thoughts and just breathe. It is very important as you serve others at home and at work to take care of you.*

# *Change Your Perception*

*Magic is the art of illusion. The idea is someone uses sleight of hand to trick your eyes to see and mind to believe what they are doing is real. That they indeed sawed a woman in half and then reattached her. Cleanly at that. Whether you believe in magic or you do not the fact is the world is filled with it. How else would you explain that feeling you get when something simple happens that makes your entire day? How do you begin to break down the idea of falling in love? Even better what would your excuse be to explain the beauty and wonder of nature? Magic exists and the more you believe it the easier it is to see. It is in a child's laugh and in a tender kiss. It is in the air that blows through the trees. You cannot see the wind, but you can surely feel it. You cannot touch a soul, but you know when it connects to yours. The universe is filled with wonders and amazement if you let your mind run free. As a child you ran and played in the rain. You had no worries of what rain was or where did it come from.*

## Change Your Perception

*You played in the snow yet never gave notice to the fact that the snow was the same rain just frozen. The fact is we lose our inner child as we grow up. Troubled relationships and choices cause a film over it that makes it tough to let loose. Then as if that were not enough you are told by society to act your age. Follow the path. Go to school, get a job, get married, have children, then die. Be mature people say or better yet act your age not your shoe size. That little girl or boy gets locked away and never gets let out to play. The people who never lose their inner child though. They are truly magic in human form. They can laugh hysterically at an inappropriate joke. They will still play in a storm or make snow angels. They love like it is the first and last time every single time. Paying no attention to the scars that choice leaves. They dance when the music hits and sing when the mood strikes. We could all take pointers from these society weirdos. You see the weirdos as they are labeled are the ones truly living life.*

## Change Your Perception

*They may not show up on the radar of importance to the world, but they are typically the people you never forget. Whether they pass on to share their joy in another time or move to new location. They leave an impact you may never truly notice until you let your child out. So, to all my fellow weirdos of the world salute. Thank you for the magic you bring in everyone's life. Even if they don't want it. Best believe they need it. Keep bringing your passion into this cold and dark world. For as a ship needs a lighthouse to guide it to shore in the fog. So does society need you to lead it from the darkness with your unique glow.*

# Change Your Perception

*Is the glass half full or half empty? The age-old question only slightly less popular than what came first the chicken or the egg. Optimist will tell you the glass is half full. While pessimists will say the glass is obviously half empty. The even more interesting view comes from science where it is said the glass is always full. You see where the liquid ends the air begins meaning the glass is actually full. It is all about perception. How you see things and their surroundings will control your judgment. If you think negatively in most situations, you would be the pessimist. If you are constantly positive than you would obviously be the optimist. Why not be both? Side with science and see things as full? The more you challenge your brain to see more then the obvious. The more in tune you are with your surroundings.*

# Change Your Perception

*Anyone can have a good idea. Many an invention started as a wild thought. Not everyone though will do the work to bring that idea to fruition. Toil tirelessly mentally, physically, and emotionally to change a dream into a reality. That is what separates society. We are all thinkers and dreamers. Our heads in the clouds daydreaming of the next big thing. Most of us though ignore the work necessary to make our dreams our reality. There by relegating ourselves to the famous phrase "I had that same idea years ago." The difference is the one claiming the fame and fortune did the work. Lost the sleep and missed the meals. Put energy into your thoughts and make your dreams your reality.*

## Change Your Perception

*Mind control is the act of dominating a weak-minded person or people. Tricking them into believing something that benefits the originators goals. The followers of society who are too afraid to lead are unfortunately the majority. Those are the targets. They will ignorantly support whatever someone of stature tells them is true. Strengthen your mind. Do not fall in line with the followers. Be a leader. Though it may not be a lavish lifestyle. It offers you the freedom to think and do outside the boundaries of society. Learn all you can learn. Read all you can read. Prepare yourself for the revolution of stupidity coming towards you. If this world had more people willing to intelligently lead. We would not be in the situations we find ourselves in. Remember we are doomed to repeat history because we refuse to learn from it. Not only in society but also in our personal lives. Learn from failure and mistakes. They often teach you way more the success. Then apply them to your surroundings. Be the change the world needs. Not another problem it cannot fix.*

# Change Your Perception

*All those times you thought you were not good enough you really were.*

*All those times you thought you were not beautiful you were beautiful all along.*

*All those times you felt inferior to someone there was someone feeling inferior to you.*

*We are all perfectly imperfect. The things you put so much stake in are just perceptions. Your perceptions of yourself or others will never be the same to someone else. Love who you are and know anything that needs to be changed. Well, those are your choices so you can love yourself more. Never sell yourself out for anyone else. Know that no matter what you do you will never be everything to everyone. Be everything to you. That is the only one that matters.*

# *Change Your Perception*

*The world changes*

*It continues to spin*

*Wars constantly raging*

*Love will always win*

*The clouds my darken*

*The ground may shake*

*The battles raging on*

*Still, we will not break*

# *Change Your Perception*

*In the times of great tragedy, we see the humanity in people. We watch as all races and creeds band together to build on united front. Giving all, they can to support those effected most by whatever may have happened.*

*Stop right there! Think and reread. Pause and collect your thoughts. Then move forward.*

*Why do we wait until life-or-death situations to band together? Why do needless deaths need to occur or acts of nature to destroy in order to be one? Why is it so hard every day to just love one another the way we were created to do?*

*Stop right there! Ponder the questions and then look in the mirror. Ask yourself why and then answer. You are only accountable for yourself, but still all the same accountable. Think on that and find the answers within, and then be the solution. Be the example instead of part of the problem.*

## Change Your Perception

*Every beginning is another beginning's end. Things always change. When you do not adapt or change with them. That is when disappointment hits you.*

## Change Your Perception

*The heart hears differently than the brain. It communicates with a language and cyphers the brain does not fully understand. I think that is why they always say listen to your heart.*

## *Change Your Perception*

*Change your habits:*

*Take time to enjoy the little things in life. Finding joy in everyday things gives you more moments to look forward to. So, when you are having a bad day there is always something to brighten your spirits.*

## Change Your Perception

*Stop looking for magic from outside sources and start looking in the mirror. Your thoughts and words carry more power than you know. You've slept on yourself long enough. It is time to wake up to your greatness and most authentic self. Always follow your intuition and listen to your heart. Do not let people who did not follow their dreams keep you from following yours. Keep the inner child alive and all its wonder and adventure. Embrace you in all your uniqueness and splendor. The right people will always find you at the right time.*

## Change Your Perception

*Just think. The thought you just had is now the past. That is how fast time flies....*

## *Change Your Perception*

*Love knows no bounds or limits. It is unaware of time or situations. It does not care where you are or what your plans are. Love is infinite and all encompassing. Much like time and space love continues well beyond our minds ability to comprehend. It is pure and true. It comes in and takes you completely by surprise. Then it changes your life completely in just an instant.*

## Change Your Perception

*People do not understand silence. They cower in fear from it. They assume something is wrong, and maybe something is. Silence is necessary to understand oneself. If you are constantly speaking, you are missing too many details. Stop and listen. More is said in silence than ever will be in the open. Let silence be one of your languages. Speak it fluently. See clearly what you are missing. It may help you understand what you are struggling to make sense of.*

## Change Your Perception

*Be wary as you place your flower down to pursue the options of the field. What was easily discarded by you maybe another's perfect gift.*

*CB*

## Change Your Perception

*Funny how quickly we rush into love with someone else. Yet we struggle mightily for most of our lives to fall in love with ourselves. Should not self-love be what we choose to rush into? How many people have come and gone in your life that you rushed feelings for? How often in your life have you come and gone out of your life? Take a second to think on that. It typically takes ninety days for someone to show who they really are. That is why so many jobs give a ninety-day probation period. Yet people are out here professing true love after a couple weeks. Never once saying I love myself. You are standing in your own way of progress. The universe has had a plan for you all along. The one has been on their journey to you all along. Most likely held up by their own ridiculous mistakes. What you need to do is spend all the wasted time on others and place it on you. Learn to love yourself fully. Focus solely on you and as you do the universe will put everything in place. Exactly as it is supposed to be there.*

## Change Your Perception

*Speak your wants positively into the universe and then focus on you. See how quickly your desires are brought to fruition. Look at it like this. When you are staring at a clock waiting to go home from work it seems like forever. Yet if you stay vigilantly working finishing time seems to fly up on you. Same goes for your personal life. Work tirelessly on what is most important that being you and see how quickly it all falls into place. Compared to focusing on everyone else staring at the clock. Wishing and wondering when it is going to be my turn. Minutes passing like days and days passing like years. You can't love anyone fully until you fully love yourself. Flip the script and change the perception.*

## Change Your Perception

*There is nothing either good or bad but thinking makes it so.*

*William Shakespeare*

*Your Perception may not be my reality.*

*Aporva Kala*

## Change Your Perception

*Intuition comes very close to clairvoyance. It appears to be the extrasensory perception of reality.*

*Alexis Carrel*

*There are always two people in every picture. The photographer and the viewer.*

*Ansel Adams*

## Change Your Perception

*Shhhhh.... They are solving all their problems and curing all their sadness.*

## Change Your Perception

*When life seems upside down change your perception.*

## Change Your Perception

*Change your habits:*

*Practice smiling. You have so much to smile about. You are here and so many are not. You have a place to sleep. Food to eat. You can find something to smile about every day.*

# Change Your Perception

*Healing is difficult. It looks different to each person. There is no timetable. Ignoring it or avoiding it does nothing but start the chase. You see no matter how fast you may run those demons will catch up. Remember as a kid your teacher screaming do not run in the halls? We all smacked our lips and rolled our eyes. Then out of nowhere someone falls and proves the words, someone's going to get hurt right? That advice still holds true. When you run no matter in what capacity it's an innate reaction to look back. That is when the stumble happens. You break sight of what is in front of you and before you can re-adjust. Bam! You have hit a hole. That few seconds is all your problems needed to catch up. Then they pile up on you until you feel like you are suffocating. Take your time and move at your own pace. Remember to breathe and that it's one step at a time. One day at a time. Hurt as you need and cry when you want to. Human emotions are a beautiful thing. It's what separates us from the machines.*

## Change Your Perception

*The answers you seek are all around you.*

*Be still and listen don't just hear.*

*Look past what your eyes perceive. Fear not the challenge of change.*

*Most importantly be willing to accept. For when we are open to the truth.*

*The truth can and will set your soul free.*

## Change Your Perception

*All too often it's the ones you would never expect struggling the most. Through fake smiles and forced persona's they try their best to fade in. Just to feel normal and not so overwhelmed by the madness inside. Broken dreams, broken hearts, and broken attempts at normality. Most their time spent in a self-inflicted darkness. Alone and afraid to take a hand of help. The fear of being okay just as scary if not more than the darkness. The darkness that has become home. Knowing that every break could be the last one. Much like any other addiction it only takes one time to push you over the edge. Spilling those famous phrases. I'm okay. I'm just really busy. I can pull myself out. I just don't want to burden anyone else.*

*It may always look different, but the reality is always the same.*

# *Change Your Perception*

*Perception is everything. What you see as small, others see as big.*

*So. When you feel small and insignificant remember. There are smaller things that see you as huge.*

*When you feel huge there is always something bigger than you. You are perfectly you and no one can ever be you.*

*Nor can you ever be someone else. Why would you want to be?*

## *Change Your Perception*

*La beauté n'est que perception. Ce que vous considérez comme beau, les autres ne le seront peut-être pas. Il en va de même pour la perfection. Ainsi, au lieu de vous efforcer d'obtenir des choses perspicaces, soyez simplement vous-même, car vous seul êtes la chose la plus belle et la plus parfaite au monde.*

*Translation:*

*Beauty is just perception. What you see as beautiful others may not. The same goes for perfection. So instead of striving for perceptive things just be you, because just you is the most beautiful and perfect thing in the world.*

# Change Your Perception

*You look out the same window and see the same tree. Year after year you see the seasons change looking slightly to the side. You see the leaves change from vibrant green to red and yellow. Before seeing them fall to the ground below. You struggle to see around it to the park on the other side. Then happenstance brings your lease to an end. Moving you across the park into a new building. Now as you peer out of your window you see clearly the scenery you once missed. In the distance you see this tree in the perfect location. Its canopy perfect shade to have a picnic or read a book. Located just shy of the creek and far enough away from the public eating area. As you walk across the street you nestle into the trunk of the tree. Begin to open your book and then look up. You see something you have seen one hundred times before. A branch in the shape of a fork. You look slightly to the left to see your old building. Perception is everything. If you had taken the walk earlier, you would have had that same spot all along. There are always at least two sides to everything. Nothing is ever exactly as it seems. When you choose to see all sides, you then become more educated about the situation. Laziness gets you nothing but mediocracy. Strive for greatness in all you do.*

## *Change Your Perception*

*Memories are forever.*

*Things change, and people come and go.*

*Oh, but those memories. They linger and stay with us all our days.*

*Stories caught in a photograph. Emotions wrapped into a song. Though the brain may slip in age you always find the memories.*

*Those moments captured in stills you will never forget. Live for the memories. Make them as often as you can.*

*File them away for those rainy days where everything seemingly goes wrong.*

# *Change Your Perception*

*Return to nature and connect to the elements from where you were created. We are all earth being our bones. Fire in the passion and drive we possess. Air in our lungs to give us life. Water making up vital biochemical existences like blood. Space or sky well we are created from both. Explains the twinkle in an eye or the constant need to look up as we daydream. We come from all that surrounds us, yet we spend more time away from it then with it. Hike a trail or climb a rock face. Sit in a park under a tree or raft a river. Get back in touch with the sights, sounds, and smells of nature. Pause and take it all in. Deep breathe in as you take the cool breeze through your nose and out of your mouth. Find a quiet place to meditate. Allowing your soul to connect to its origins. When you leave and come back to normality. You will feel a sense of grounding you have been missing. Clarity, you search everywhere for, and a desire to run back again real soon. Mother Nature is calling come home. Hearken her call and accept her invitation. You can always go home.*

## *Change Your Perception*

*Remember no matter how dark the cave is. There is always enough light for you to glow and to grow..*

## Change Your Perception

*When you're hurt. Stop and sit in silence.*

*Life is teaching you something.*

*Allow yourself to learn, so you can heal properly.*

## Change Your Perception

Change your habits:

Once a week write something nice on a piece of paper. Then as you pass someone pass it to them and keep walking.

Place it on someone's desk at work or drop it somewhere you know someone will pick up.

You do not know what people are going through and one little phrase could change their direction.

Talk them off the ledge or bring raw emotion to the surface. Not to mention if they pay it forward.

You will never know what impact that thirty seconds of your time had.

## Change Your Perception

*Slippery when wet. The warning sign to slow down as road conditions are such that excessive speed could lead to you losing control. Leading to a potentially fatal crash. Isn't that life though? When you think, speak, and act in a fast manner or as we would call it reactive. You tend to do so chaotically. Sending you slipping and sliding out of control into the walls of your brain. Crashing with wheels spinning having no clue how to save yourself. Hoping someone else will come along and see your warning signs or flashers blinking. Stop and pull over to offer just a little help. Look at it this way. You are driving down an interstate. You like everyone else are doing five to ten miles per hour over the posted limit. I mean who does not?*

## *Change Your Perception*

Someone flies by you as you cruise at optimal speed doing twenty miles per hour over the limit. Paying no attention to the fact one slight hiccup and they could lose complete control of their vehicle. Risking the lives of every person traveling that road. Funny thing is as they leave you as a blip in the rear-view mirror. You come up on the exit to see that car waiting just like you. They were in such a hurry to sit and wait. Making it there no more than thirty seconds before you. Practice patience knowing regardless of where you are going you will get there. Going faster and losing control just prolongs your journey. Plus look at all the things you miss not moving at a steady pace. Your self-health is critical as there are so many counting on you in life.

# Change Your Perception

You may feel alone but really if you have a job your coworkers and boss count on you to show up every day. If you have a family and kids, you know you are counted on more than maybe you care to be at times. Your life means more to people than you may think. Maybe you are just spinning out of control on the wet streets of life. Stop. Take a few deep breaths. Take your time. One day at a time and one step at a time. You are still going to make it to the same place. It is just when you finally make it you will have loads of memories to tell once you arrive.

## Change Your Perception

*What you perceive is a broken and discarded flower. There is more than what is on the surface. In the hands of the right person. That flower can be replanted and nursed back to life. Placed into a garden to thrive better than ever. The same fact goes for us. With the right care anyone can be replanted and nurtured. Becoming more than then they were before they were broken and discarded. Perception is everything*

# Change Your Perception

*Rise up out of your bed. When you would rather stay there instead.*

*Rise up off of the ground. No matter how many times you are knocked down.*

*Rise like the sun in the sky. Do not let the day get away or your time to pass by.*

*Rise to every occasion and goal. Bringing success and pride to the mind also your soul.*

*Rise like the moon in the night. Stay focused and strong in the face of the fight.*

*You can do anything with your eyes on the prize. No matter what it will take just never give up and just rise.*

## Change Your Perception

*The best way to learn how to be happy with or without other people. Is to start enjoying your own company. Then it becomes a want to be surrounded not a need.*

*PA*

## Change Your Perception

*You see the sunset and admire the beautiful colors. Watch as the sun fades into the background colliding with the skyline. Just before the moon rises from its slumber to be our evening nightlight.*

*That moment when all the colors we know and can perceive make a pallet any artist would love to paint with. It shows us clearly if we pay attention that even endings can be beautiful. Just as the day ends to become night and soon the night will fade into similar colors of dawn break. One end will always be another's beginning.*

# Change Your Perception

*Look out over the ledge and look at the depths of the fall. Only then will you truly appreciate the work of the climb to get there.*

## Change Your Perception

Nirvana, a place of perfect peace and happiness.

The highest consciousness you can reach.

Lives inside each of us.

Stop searching externally for what has been inside you all along.

## Change Your Perception

*As a writer I compose start middle end. I breathe the words to life then hit send. If the start is where we begin after all. The end must be where we finish this fall. Still if the end is where we start once more. Then it shouldn't gain the dislike or our abhorrence. It appears the middle stays the same. In this circle of life and this eternal game. It's what we remember and what matters most. Just as we remember the party never the host. So, stop focusing on the first and the last. Worry about now not the future or the past. Do whatever it is now. Please do not wait as tomorrow may not come and /or may be way too late.....*

# Change Your Perception

## Change your habits:

Before you go to sleep every night. Tell yourself that you did a great job today. It is true not everything may have gone as planned, but you made it through the day. That is reason to celebrate. Leaving your brain in a state of fulfillment as you drift off to sleep. Let go of everything that went wrong or you did not accomplish. Those things are now the past and need not come with you into tomorrow. Breathe and let yourself let go so you may sleep peacefully and be refreshed in the morning.

# Change Your Perception

*Upon each elevation comes a new revelation.*

*Everything you think you know will be seen in a different light.*

*The universe giving you a fresh insight.*

*The mystery of it will unfold and truths will be told.*

*Only the awoken will see. Some may even call you crazy.*

*They just cannot see your reality. It's okay, it's your journey to be everything you are meant to be.*

*People may not understand but that is all part of plan.*

*Some people have to fall away. If they stay, they would only be in the way.*

*The revelations lead to greater elevations, so you can see reality.*

*AM*

## *Change Your Perception*

*May the bridge between where you are and where you are going always be love.*

## Change Your Perception

*Daybreak......*

*The new beginning you have been looking for.*

*So, what are you waiting for?*

## *Change Your Perception*

*You are not out of anyone's league. They may be on a different level, but never out of reach. Saying they are too good for you is either a coping mechanism or an excuse.*

*Coping for the fact of your lack of self-confidence or your lack of self-esteem.*

*Excuse because you refuse to make necessary changes to your make up to better yourself. Instead of saying I cannot or I will never. Do the work. Climb the ladders and achieve the goals required to reach the level you desire to be on. Become the standard not the exception.*

# *Change Your Perception*

*So many people fear the darkness. Ignoring the fact that without it we would have no light. Everything in life has a counterbalance. Running from one side only makes you less in the other. Joy comes with sadness. Stability only comes through instability. You are both your dark and your light. With great sadness and depression comes great happiness. It may take time and hard work, but as you have heard nothing worth having comes easy. When in the deepest darkness it is impossible to see the light. Not because it does not exist, but because you choose to focus on the dark. Ignoring the light that has been there all along. It is imperative that you practice perception. Seeing all that surrounds you can save you a plunge that needs not happen. If you walk down the street never looking down, you are destined to step in a pothole. Yet if you occasionally look downward as you walk you are prepared for anything in your path that can trip you up. Just remember even beauty grows in the darkness. Some of the most beautiful flowers only bloom at night.*

# *Change Your Perception*

*The heart is the epicenter of your spiritual energy. When you love you release positive vibes and energy. Your aura glows brighter and you become infectious. Leading people to seek that happiness you are exuding. Be the vibration those around you need. Become the beacon of energy and light this world needs.*

## Change Your Perception

*Danger is very present, but fear is a choice.*

*Make sure you know the difference.*

*Do not let fear drive you away from your success.*

*Stay vigilant and ever changing.*

*Great things do not happen by chance.*

## *Change Your Perception*

*Never be afraid of the adventure. If you never allow yourself to get lost, then you will never truly find yourself. It is always in the most unexpected places that you find the greatest rewards.*

## Change Your Perception

When you think you are facing an unclimbable mountain. Instead of negatively thinking about the work ahead. Change your perception. Think of the positive that will come out of your success. Maybe it was never about the climb. Maybe the universe put the mountain in front of you to show others it could be scaled. That with positive energy and belief that mountain could be moved. If you can dream it you can do it and if you believe in it you can make it so. You can achieve anything which you put your mind to.

## Change Your Perception

*Slow down and allow yourself to be more aware of your surroundings. Taste your food and take in the scents that spark a memory. Listen to those songs that remind you of days past. It is okay to hurt it is how we heal. It is okay to cry. We are humans and our emotions are a gift. Remember your past in vivid colors and details. Remember those details, places, and people that have molded you into your perfectly imperfect self. Nostalgia will allow you to not only remember the good times, but to be thankful for the bad times that have come and gone. Look for the moments that take your breath away. Then remember the way you felt and what you saw. So, as life tries to fly by you have those moments to escape to. Do this regularly and I promise you will never see the memories same again.*

*PA*

## Change Your Perception

*Change your habits:*

*Stop....*

*Think....*

*Listen....*

*Feel....*

*Center....*

*Breathe....*

*Then attack...*

*Be cerebral in your methods and actions. More importantly in control of your reactions.*

## Change Your Perception

Words I have found are the most dangerous weapons one person can wield.

One sentence can both tear down a life and also build one up.

Words have the ability to leave scars no one can see and some that one may never heal from.

Be patient to speak and be sure of the meaning of what you say. Once those syllables leave your tongue, you cannot take them back. The wound you leave may prove to cause a hemorrhage no tourniquet can stop.

## Change Your Perception

*It's a shame more people choose to lead with their egos rather than their hearts. Heads bigger than the door they try to enter. Your brain is the epicenter of the body. All the commands coming from it. You rarely hear I hurt my brain. Leading with your heart would of course be more painful. Yet pain is an emotion and a reaction from the brain. Our emotions are meant to be felt. It keeps us separate from the machines. To set one's ego to the side is a sign of humility. The lovers of the world tend to have suffered the most for the reason of leading with the heart. Those who show no humility and just speak whatever their ego says. They are the issue with society. Too hardnosed to love because they got hurt. Then decided I'm going to make sure no one is ever as stupid as I was.*

## *Change Your Perception*

*They still love masked under sarcasm. The care behind veils of criticism. Instead of just loving and relegating themselves to always healing. Still, those who do constantly heal also constantly learn. They grow and change. Everything this world needs.*

*Growth, change, and to learn from mistakes. Rather than a society filled with anger and arrogance that follows the same old paths that have not and will never work.*

*Heads like hot air balloons filled with bad judgment and even more cynicism to tear down any progress. Love will always defeat hate. It has since the dawn of man and will way beyond the end of man.*

## *Change Your Perception*

*Life is love. The biggest flaw people have is forcing everything into life. We are supposed to focus on every day separately.*

*If you let it the universe will weed out the bad and put what you need in your path. To run headfirst into.*

*If you constantly put someone in your life because you are lonely it will fail.*

*The right one will come when you stop deciding you are bigger, smarter, and more evolved than a universe that is infinite.*

## Change Your Perception

*Funny how as a child we play and pretend like we are adults. Seeking to grow up so fast. Yet as an adult we dream like a child and wish we could go back to those days. Leaving the responsibilities of adulthood behind for summer days playing outside and naps anytime we got sleepy. Funny how in each cycle we wish we were the other when in fact we are both all the time. We have the adult natures in us as a child and it is the parent's job to nurture them, so we grow up properly. Hopefully skewing us from the stupid and hurtful mistakes they made at our age. As adults we are still kids inside. We get excited at the things we love. We dance in the rain and our sense of humor is a direct reflection of that child that never grew up. We have always been both but as adults we choose to repress the inner child. The entity that makes life most exciting. Let your inner child out to play and see just how fun life can truly be. We have the best of both worlds. The ability to be in control of our lives and make our own decisions, and to be able to have fun doing it all. It does not have to be one or the other.*

## Change Your Perception

*Don't sacrifice your growth for someone else's acceptance.*

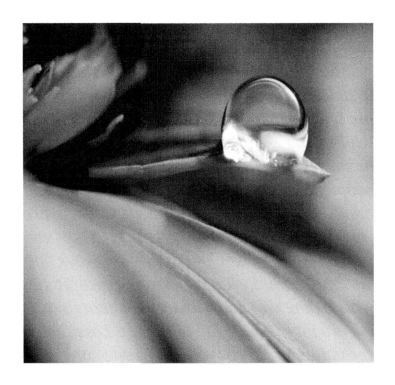

# *Change Your Perception*

*Kindness is a virtue. We have all heard this most of our lives. Yet it has become an extinct virtue. Left in its place self-centered actions and it is all about me attitude. We focus on frivolous things like money, popularity, and beauty. All these and so many more replaceable items that will eventually fade. We throw each other under the bus for a promotion that gives us more money. Then complain about the hours expected or the responsibility that is solely on us. We choose to needlessly buy with the attitude if I do not use it or need it, I will just throw it out. All the while there is a staggering growth of homelessness. We walk by down on their luck people and scoff while saying degrading things. Forgetting most of them where were we are, and misfortune struck. That can happen to anyone at any time. We always find ourselves blindly in the wrong place at the wrong time way more than the alternative. It takes a moment for life to change. Less than a second can start your uprising or your downfall. Before you can catch your breath, you can have it all or nothing. Kindness and love though are things that regardless of your place still are the exact same.*

# *Change Your Perception*

*Actually, the person you step on as you climb the ladder or spit on as beneath you show more of both than anyone else. As humility has made them humble, and they have experienced the rock bottom that they have fallen to. They know the pain and the struggle of being at the lowest points and they still choose kindness and love. I once heard two people simultaneously. A businessman whose ego was bigger than the wallet he bragged about. Counting all the meaningless things he could and did buy. Talking negatively about the people who surely where the reason for his success. While at the same time I heard one of those employees talking about how grateful they were to even have a job. How they could finally buy their daughters prom dress. How great a man this leader was even if he was just a number to the bottom line. The complete disparity between arrogance and humility was shocking. One grateful for the man who disgracefully talked about the same person singing his praises. The moral of the story is that kindness is in all of us as is love. In the end no one will remember your accomplishments, what you owned, or how much you made.*

## Change Your Perception

*You will fade as a memory as life continues without your presence. In your place someone else doing more and at half the cost while making more than you did. What they will remember is how you treated people and how you made them feel. Memories are never about how rich or famous you were. They are always about what kind of impression and impact you made not on your own life, but on the millions of others around you. You may not think you matter or are insignificant, but that is far from the truth. You impact hundreds of people every day. From family and friends to the people around you as you drive. Your co-workers and the people you pass walking down the street. That person you did not know but still you chose to wave at. They may be at rock bottom and that wave made them feel like too were worthy of being noticed. Even for just a moment. Which brings us back to how life can change in just a moment.*

## *Change Your Perception*

*When you finally realize the race, you are running is not against time. It is against yourself. That's the moment you actually start to live.*

# *Change Your Perception*

*Change your habits:*

*Instead of immediately responding be it conversation in person or through message. Take five minutes to center. Think about the words. Is it worth the energy to respond in haste or anger? It is so much easier to say I will be right back give me a minute then to spew venom that will never be forgotten. The words may fade but the scars will remain. Be slow to respond and to judge. A lot can happen in a few minutes. Make sure you did not take their words wrong. Think about the most productive words to respond. Ask the important questions that defuse. Your moments will also give the other side the opportunity to reflect. You lose so much energy and peace in strife and anger. With no positive result. You are left stewing as are they and no real progress is ever made.*

# *Change Your Perception*

*Slow down you are not winning the race. You are just missing so much moving at a break necks pace.*

*Take your time and see the sights. Smell the roses or watch as butterflies and birds change their flights.*

*Take a deep breath in and then out. Take in the energy and peace that a positive life is all about.*

*It is about the journey not the destination. When you run non-stop to the end your present you diminish.*

*Leaving all your possible smiles relegated to a frown. You can change your perception and all of this once you simply slow down.*

# Change Your Perception

*You should never have to tell someone how to love you. Love is an innate core feeling. When someone truly loves you, they will never not know how to tell or show you. It may not look or sound like what you are used to. Accept the fact that you have allowed too many to fool you with four letters. Everyone's language is different. The most exciting part of all relationships regardless of their nature is learning someone's language. Some may speak in poetry while others in songs. There are those that compliment yet can never take one in return. Some may speak in touch or in affection. You cannot expect to receive what you refuse to put in. If you are having to consistently correct or navigate someone to love. They do not love you they love the idea of you. They love your mannerisms or words. Your looks or what you can provide. That is not loving you. Anyone can give them what they seek and that is why once you stop accepting it, they are moving on to the next one. Letting go is as simple as accepting the truth.*

# *Change Your Perception*

*The more you make excuses or lie to yourself to cover the facts. The longer your journey to heal is. People come and they go in life. All playing the role the universe had in mind for them. Holding them on the page knowing the next chapter they will not play a part. Delays your story because it is still being written. You are just falling behind, each day missing the things on those pages you had to skip to catch up. You are doing yourself a disservice no one else. Those people you cling to have moved on with their story. Coming back to fill double spaces in the paragraphs because you will not move on. They know they can come back to find you standing still like a confused statue. Stop being a filler because of your own fear and insecurities. You are the main character of your story not a supporting actor to someone else's. Why settle for the special thanks page when you can be the plot of your own book?*

# *Change Your Perception*

*Changing your perception is as easy as changing the words.*

*Instead of saying I have a dream say I have a plan.*

*Instead of saying tomorrow say today, because every day is another's tomorrow.*

*Instead of saying I wish say I am going to. Knowing it will take time but so does waiting on a wish to come true.*

*Instead of being the excuse be the exception.*

*Instead of saying I am sorry show you are and then change your mannerisms. Apologies are not excuses for actions they are opportunities to change.*

*Perception is all in how you see it. Changing your perception gives access to growth and change.*

## *Change Your Perception*

*Always believe something great is about to happen. Releasing positive energy and vibes into the universe will manifest the same in return. If your day is going wrong instead of focusing solely on the negative stop and assess. The more negativity you put into manifestation the more you obtain in return. Look at those days where everything seems to fall your way. You saw one thing and stayed positive all day and so that's what you kept receiving. Same goes for the bad. As one bad thing happened you kept seeing negative and anything that could go wrong seemed to. Be mindful of what you think and speak. If you challenge the universe by saying things like what is the worst that can happen. You will soon find out more than you care to know.*

## *Change Your Perception*

*When you tear the veil of reality and change your perception. You allow yourself to finally see beyond just what your eyes see. That's when your journey can truly begin.*

# Change Your Perception

Everyone is always looking for the big things to happen. Completely ignoring all the small things that add together to make the big results. Always impatient and unable to wait for the timing to be right. We complain that it is not happening fast enough. Take the time to appreciate the little things that make life great. One leaf does not make a tree. It takes thousands of little leaves to make a canopy. It also takes the supporting factors like the wood and trunk. The roots and the nutrients those roots bring to feed the leaves. Every big thing is made of up of many small pieces to make a complete puzzle. Instead of being focused on the big promotion focus on the small details that will make you the irreplaceable and valuable candidate. The work that you do and the help you give to progress not only you but your co-workers. The time you spend when no one else would or the extra functions you do not have to do but choose to.

# Change Your Perception

*All those little details paint the big picture and will lead to success faster than grumbling and complaining it is not happening fast enough. Looking for love well instead of falling in love when you feel you should wait until you are ready. Let all the smaller pieces fall into place. Allow yourself to properly heal and to learn to not need someone to exist. Then when you least expect, it love comes walking in. It will not be the work load you have become accustomed to. It will be as it should be. Effortless and beautiful. Those small things become the memories on the reel of your life. The things you will always remember. You never just give the ending to a movie or book. You give the details that make others want to read or watch it. You will never remember the big endings. You will however passionately explain all the smallest details that lead to them.*

## *Change Your Perception*

*A great person can have a great idea. A great mind though can change the world greatly.*

## Change Your Perception

*When bound in your darkness clinging to the strings of your sanity. Struggling to see light or resolution. You will find your balance and serenity. If you sit in the silence, you will realize you are both the light and the darkness completely yet neither entirely.*

## Change Your Perception

*Change your habits:*

*Instead of trying to figure everything out all at once. Focus on just one thing. Start small and dig into the issue. Find the root of why you cannot let it go and then make a plan of attack. No army on history ran into war without some sort of plan. Success or failure they always had an idea of how to win. Solve one problem at a time allowing yourself to free yourself from it. Giving the brain space to handle the next issue with more space to function. Starting a bunch of projects at once yet finishing none does not ever show the effort put in. Start and finish one at a time and slowly you will find less tying you to sleeplessness.*

## Change Your Perception

*Stay dedicated nothing happens overnight. If you find that to be false, take a step back. You have been doing the work slowly in the background like the apps you never close out on your phone. If you ask for something and it immediately happens then you have been walking to the perfect place all along. Your timing is not impeccable it is expected. You have not focused on the important things that got you there. Most likely wandering focused on everything other then what you finally realized you needed. Being vigilant and dedicated to your goals will always bring the results of success. If you are not finding that make sure you are looking at the right goals. You get everything you need in life not everything you want, when you find yourself getting what you wanted you also needed it. The universe is never wrong no matter how many times you swear it is. Everything happens as it is supposed to and when it is supposed to.*

## Change Your Perception

*While you put so much emphasis on those criticizing everything you do. Stop and remember. The people doing more than you or at the very least the same as you never criticize. They are too busy making themselves better and stronger. The ones that are trying to derail you with negativity are the ones who are doing less than you or nothing. Trying to take away from the fact they will not keep up. It is never a matter of cannot it is always the fact of will not. So, ignore the haters and tell yourself regularly. I must be the best tasting thing in the world, because they cannot seem to keep me out of their mouths. Keep climbing and never let anyone take you off your level unless they are bringing you up to theirs.*

# Change Your Perception

*Where will you be in a year? How about six months? What about two months? Will you still be in the same place talking about where you want to go and what you want to do? Will you be somewhere completely different on your journey? The choice is yours and yours alone. You can prepare for success all your life but never do a thing to achieve it. Sure, you may find your luck is up into a few great things along the way, but you will fall way short of the greatest rewards of life. When others talk about you will they say oh, yeah him or her? They are always saying they are going to do this or that. Yet they are still here talking and going nowhere. Will they sing your praises and say oh, him or her? You should see them now. Completely different person.*

# Change Your Perception

*Took them some hard work and a lot of time but man did they finally make it. It is all about planning and effort. Setting small achievable goals as well as big ones that those other goals will feed into. You will fall and fail we all do. You will get cuts and scrapes. Beaten up and bruised but you will proceed. Keep your head down consistently focused on your own self wealth, self-growth, and most importantly self-health. Taking care of you will always bring the results of success. Once again remember, one day at a time and one step at a time will always equal to one success at a time and one milestone at a time.*

## Change Your Perception

*You may not be ready for everything you will go through or have gone through in life. We never are prepared for the roadblocks and potholes that throw us off course. As unready as you may think you are, you were built to go through it. Everything we endure is another step closer to the rewards waiting for us when we are finished. Even a flower is built to serve its purpose. As soft and delicate as they may seem. They still grow in the elements and survive the storms to become fragrant and beautiful. They create the oxygen we breathe in, and the pollen needed for the bees to do their jobs in the course of nature.*

## Change Your Perception

*They will eventually be beautiful in an arrangement for both celebration and grief. Then when it seems their purpose is fulfilled, they are dried out and become some of the sweetest smelling potpourri. We like the flower have a never-ending cycle of growth and rebirth to make in every lifetime we exist. Constantly changing to adapt to the elements we face. Growing into full form and serving whatever our purpose is until we succeed and head back to all we derived from.*

## Change Your Perception

*You cannot become better by always remaining the same. Results come from change it does not come from fear of failure. You miss one hundred percent of the shots you never take.*

## Change Your Perception

*Do not fear failure. Fear being the same every day. Fear not changing as the world changes around you. Fear never feeling the satisfaction of hard work and perseverance.*

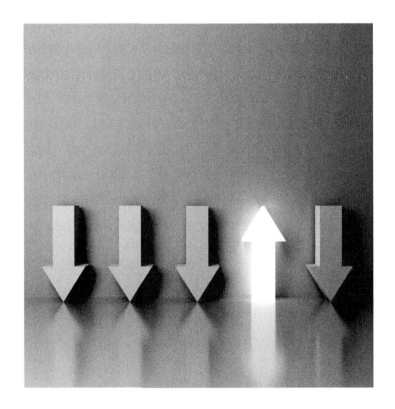

## Change Your Perception

*Respect yourself enough to cut the toxic out of your life. You owe it to nobody to keep any person or thing that brings negativity into your life. Cutting ties does not make you a bad person. It means you value yourself enough to not let controllable things destroy the life you are working hard to build. If it does not add to your growth, it is toxic. Realize what needs to be removed before it infects the foundation of your building. This goes not only for your personal life but also for your professional life. You cannot control how others act but you do control how you react as well as how much you interact. Always put yourself first. You are not a doormat for everyone to walk over. You are the house they seek to occupy rather than fixing the one they chose to destroy.*

# Change Your Perception

*Pick your battles wisely. Not every war is worth fighting. Especially the one you wage daily with yourself. Imploding from inside and dealing with self-induce abuse only leaves you welcoming it from an outside source. How can you begin to trust anyone if you do not trust yourself? How will you ever truly love if you hate yourself? You can never fully teach or expect that which you do not fully known. You are doing yourself and everyone else an injustice. Love you more than anyone or anything else. Stop picking fights with yourself. Understand you are a flawed individual prone to failure. It will happen multiple times a day. Be kind and forgive yourself and learn from the mistakes. Self-growth is imperative to any kind of successes in life.*

## Change Your Perception

*Change your habits:*

*List daily all your successes and read them over and over.*

*Train your brain to let go of the failures that hinder your mental strength.*

*Focusing on the successes breeds more success. It instills positivity and more importantly trains the brain to transfer from negative to positive in any situation.*

## Change Your Perception

*A life with no struggle is a life with no progress. The struggles we go through prepare us for anything we encounter in the future. We learn from it and in turn it makes us better.*

# Change Your Perception

*Your mindset should always be stronger than your emotions. Emotions tend to be chaotic and often times hard to control. Losing one's emotions can lead to anger outburst or harmful words one cannot take back. Daily we need to strengthen our minds by training them to think before speaking. Taking the time to ponder what has been said or done controls the emotional outbursts leading to the mind being in control. Like all habits changing the way you do things takes time. We are all creatures of habit. That does not mean our habits have to be bad ones. Finding things that allow you to quickly locate your center is essential. Be it a breathing technique or finding a quite spot to assess. Meditation will help you stay aligned but is not always available in times of conflict. A strong mind means a strong balance. Saving the emotions until after resolution and leaving you with a cool head in times that matter the most.*

## *Change Your Perception*

*You **should** want to succeed*

*You **would** do whatever it takes*

*You **could** just give up*

*You **did** not and found success*

## Change Your Perception

*Ninety percent of your life is a reaction. Think about that for a second. That would mean only ten percent of life is what happens to us. Makes sense though. You breathe because you die if you do not that is a reaction. You could choose not to and the reaction to that choice is loss of oxygen causing the body to fail. You can choose to not eat or drink. That is a chosen reaction as the opposite would be not to. The way you drive is a reaction to the rules of the road, the lines on the road, and the things you encounter on the roads. Every action of your day is just a reaction. You react to sleeping by waking up and vice versa. You get out of bed you then get dressed and head to work.*

## Change Your Perception

*Your attitude and everything you do is a reaction to those surrounding you. So, if life is a reaction that means all the situations, we feel out of control we are simply choosing the wrong reactions. We can choose to never let things bother us or hurt us. We can choose success and never fail. We can be and do anything we want to make our lives the best and most positive as possible. So instead of talking about what we can do let's just go out and show results.*

## Change Your Perception

*Fight on when you feel like quitting. Those who oppose you are standing strong they are not sitting.*

*Fight harder when your strength is failing. Stand firm and resilient when you feel like bailing.*

*Fight for your opinions and beliefs. The ocean does not back down as it crashes against the rock and reefs.*

*When life is its hardest and you tend to lose sight. Take a deep breath, expand your chest and just fight.*

## Change Your Perception

*You do not have to be everything to everyone. You do have to be everything to you. So, stop putting everything and everyone before you. In the end you only have you. You are there one hundred percent of the time. You should always matter the most to yourself.*

## Change Your Perception

*Rest your head and close your eyes. After you say goodnight and kiss your goodbyes.*

*Rest your body and your brain. The day has been long, and the work has caused it strain.*

*Rest your heart and your soul. You have put in the work given it your all and reached your goal.*

*You may have failed but you did your best. Tomorrows a new day so just rest.*

## Change Your Perception

*Remember as the night breaks and you unwind from whatever your day held. Tomorrow comes with the dawn. Another day and a chance for a brand-new start. There are no limits on how often you press the restart button. If you do not like something change it tomorrow. Leave yesterday in the past. Carrying it over ruins your new day. Release and rewind. That is the motto before you close your eyes to rest that beautiful brain.*

# Change Your Perception

*You don't have to force connection it just happens. Searching for things will give you false thoughts and hopes. What is meant to be will just be. You will not have to look for it. It will show itself clearly like a smack in the face. Forcing it though can leave you feeling disappointed when you feel you were wrong. Causing negativity in your energy.*

*That can be dangerous when searching for higher consciousness. Forcing things as vital as love or connections is a type of self-sabotage. The desire to be intertwined with one person can lead you down a path of heartbreak and suffering. You then begin to ignore the signs that they are not right for you. The more you lie to yourself the more damage you do.*

*When all is said and done all your feelings are reactions to your own desires and how the other person acts.*

## *Change Your Perception*

*You set yourself up for things like pain and heartbreak when you start to force powerful emotions. Let what is meant for you present itself at the time designed for it to happen. Going out looking is a defense mechanism used to fill the holes of loneliness. Instead fill those holes with the things that bring you joy and happiness. Not with others but by yourself. Prepare yourself for that perfect connection and happiness by using that time wisely. Learning to love yourself so you know how to love someone else. Connecting with yourself so you can understand what real connections feel like. Do not rush what will come naturally or you will find yourself constantly over working for something that will never last.*

## Change Your Perception

*Change your habits:*

*Look at all your mistakes and miscues of the day. Assess the damage that was done and look for how you could have done things differently. Write these things down in a journal and review them regularly. This is a method to help you learn from what did not work while releasing it from your brain. Stopping yourself from being emotionally abusive for making mistakes. All of this is growth. It is essential to constantly change to adapt your ever-changing life. Allowing yourself to read what went wrong or what was said wrong will let you see it from a different point of view. One not jumbled up with a million other things. Now formulate a plan to do things differently and make sure to chart your success too. When you eliminate the bad choices and replace them with the right ones. You effectively change negative energy into positive.*

## *Change Your Perception*

*Impatience will not make the right stuff happen faster. It will only make all the wrong ones continue to happen. Then when you are meant to be in the right situation you will be wrapped up in the wrong ones you forced. Making you wait even longer for it all to loop back around. If it ever does. Look at all the possible things you have missed tied up in what you forced. Thinking it was right or rushing for the answers you wanted. Not the ones you need or were meant to have.*

## Change Your Perception

*Ignorance is bliss and there are too many people living in euphoria. Be the exception. Be different. Do not follow the heard as they are destined for disaster. Blaze your own trail. Walk it with confidence and intelligence. Be the example everyone else wants to follow.*

## Change Your Perception

*You don't have to be perfect. Perfection is just a perception that is never the same for everyone. All you need to be is yourself. Enjoy this messy imperfect beautiful life. You will be happier for it.*

## Change Your Perception

*When you stop fearing what may go wrong and start focusing on what may go right. You will find yourself more successful and happier. Take the risk and see your rewards. Even in failure you will still succeed. The only true failure in life is to never attempt anything to start with.*

## Change Your Perception

*Avoid negative people. They will have a problem for every solution you come up with. They do not seek answers only discord.*

*Align yourself with those people who thrive on learning and live from the heart. For the heart will take you on adventures the mind is too afraid to embark on.*

*The mind sets up traps and snares to trick you into being cautious and safe. Still the heart knows the way and the coordinates to get to all the place you once only imagined.*

# Change Your Perception

*You can hear someone yet never fully listen to them.*

*You can exist yet never fully live.*

*You can be fearful yet still be brave.*

*You can have nothing yet still have everything.*

*You can dance the music never leave one spot.*

*This world and universe are full of paradoxes that you can spend your life trying to make sense of. How can one have nothing but still possess everything? It is quite simple and no need to complicate it. While having nothing of material aspects you can still have peace and joy. That being more than some that have all the lavish things money can buy.*

*A paradox is the universes way of making you see both sides of everything. By growing your perception, it also allows you to gain a higher consciousness.*

*Then you see more than what your eyes originally see. It is like watching a movie.*

## Change Your Perception

*You watch intensively because you are excited yet in focusing on the plot, so you understand the details. You have missed subtle intricacies that you will not catch until you re-watch that movie again. Sometimes more than just a few times. What is life but on big movie? It has a plot and many twists along the way. It has a main story line you follow and all along you miss the subtle details that make it so much more enjoyable. The only issue is we do not get to rewind this movie or watch it again. Once this film end and the credit's role it is on to another lifetime. So, it is vital to slow down and watch every part frame by frame. Because once that still is gone you cannot re-watch it or change it. Our journey is not to merely live and die. It is to gain the knowledge we missed in prior lifetimes. Changing the world, a little bit more every time.*

## Change Your Perception

*Your inner child is not lost you are. Look deep into the dark fog of your soul. It is still there frolicking in the trees. Just as you did when you were young.*

## *Change Your Perception*

*As time begins to slip through your fingers. As you face the end of your journey. Do not fear or worry. For with death always comes rebirth. You cannot have one without the other. We die many times life killing off older versions of ourselves. Still, we carry on new and improved.*

## Change Your Perception

*Change your habits:*

*When your brain feels overwhelmed take a few minutes and breathe. Close your eyes and focus on one thing. Keep breathing and let your mind wander with whatever you are focused on. Let it drift and feel yourself free up the needed space to operate. Open your eyes and write down what you saw. This process is called 'mindmapping.' Releasing all the details onto the paper. Then once you have finished return back to whatever you were working on.*

## Change Your Perception

*Be the positivity you seek in this world. Start every day telling yourself that positive energy is coming into my life. Changes are happening even if I cannot fully see them. Things are turning around and getting better every minute. All things are aligning as they are meant to. What I seek is right in front of me all I must do is grab it. Then as you go out into this world repeat as needed to stay the positive course.*

## *Change Your Perception*

*Remember you can always turn around. It does not matter how long or far you have traveled in the wrong direction. Change is just a complete turnaround.*

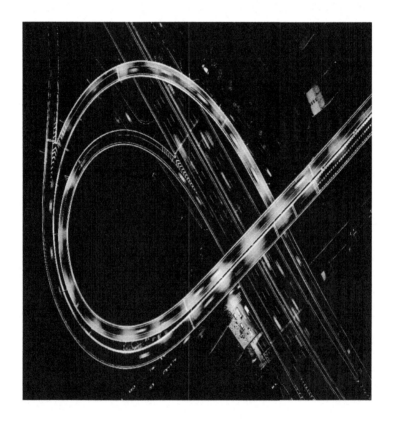

## Change Your Perception

*Do not ever judge people based on the choices they have made. You have no idea what options they had. Just as they do not know your options. We are all fighters. We have gone through our own personal hells and lived to tell the stories. No one has the same journey or faces the exact same perils. Be kind always first and foremost.*

## Change Your Perception

*Be proud of where you are and of yourself. You have made it a long way and through things you never thought you would survive. You are changing and growing every day. Appreciate your results and where you have come from. Even more so for where you are going.*

## *Change Your Perception*

*The road may be long and winding. The nights may be long and the days too short. Do not give up on the journey of life. Not today or tomorrow. Great things are just beyond the horizon, and I promise you will be grateful you never quit.*

# Change Your Perception

*Do not fall in love with a person. Fall in love with healing and growing.*

*Fall in love with yourself and where you are going.*

*Fall in love with the moments and what they all hold. Not in the things that can be bought or be sold.*

*Love your surroundings and the life you create. Put away all the doubt, negativity, and hate.*

*You are all you have and that is enough. You do not need toxic people with all of their stuff.*

*Love yourself first in all that you do. Watch how the old fades being replaced by the new.*

## *Change Your Perception*

*Strong minds discuss ideas.*
*Average minds discuss events.*
*Weak minds discuss people.*

*Socrates*

*Some people feel the rain and others just get wet.*

*Bob Marley*

## Change Your Perception

*We live in the best of all possible worlds.*

Gotfried Wilhelm Leibniz

*Raise your words not your voice. It is rain that grows flowers not the thunder.*

*Rumi*

# *Change Your Perception*

## Change Your Perception

*Special thanks to all those who contributed. Not only in work but in spirit. Some desire not to be named. If not for constant support I would be nothing.*

*Ashley Madison (written word)*

*Chris Bunton (Artwork)*

*Princess Aisha (written word)*

*Jennifer Murray (artwork)*

# Change Your Perception

Printed in Great Britain
by Amazon

37426934R00118